AGONY IN THE GARDEN

"IT WAS NO ORDINARY NIGHT"

Apostle Dr. Barbara Maybin Wise, Th.D

Published by:

Fortune Publishing Group
E-mail: info@fortunepublishinggroup.com
www.FortunePublishingGroup.com

Phone: (410) 888-0508
Printed in the United States of America

Book cover designed by Max Fortune

FOREWORD

Dr. Barbara Wise has drawn us into the very epitome of walking with Jesus on that dreadful night we celebrate as Maundy Thursday. In reading "It Was No Ordinary Night", Apostle Wise has brought such a refreshing essence of the suffering our Lord and Savior endured before being crucified on the cross. What an awesome revelation of the unending love of Christ that is revealed throughout these pages.

Dr. Apostle Wise has spent time researching the depth of Christ humility in accepting His assignment of death on the cross. This book will enlighten your spirits with heartfelt moments illustrating His untold sufferings. After reading this book "It was No Ordinary Night", you will have a greater appreciation for the cost that was paid on the cross, as well as our salvation not being taken for granted, neither will you celebrate the Resurrection of Christ (Easter) as just another religious event. Religious rituals have crept into the body of Christ having left many churches spiritually bankrupt. There is a lack of understanding concerning the agony of the cross and especially the thoughts and feelings expressed by Christ before His arrest in the Garden.

Dr. Barbara Wise is a true Woman of God that is determined to enlighten the people of God into a greater dimension of faith, while teaching God's truth with credible revelation. I am so honored to have Dr. Wise as my beautiful best friend, accountability partner and Prayer partner. Thank you, Lord, for enabling her to bring this awesome project to the kingdom for such a time as time.

May you be blessed as you spend time with the Holy Spirit reflecting on "It Was No Ordinary Night". It was a night we should always remember and one that we should be eternally grateful for.

Apostle Chiquita Clark
Restoration Anointed Worship Center
Lavonia, Georgia

PREFACE

I find myself writing this book after having spent time organizing another Good Friday service with the traditional Seven Last Sayings of Christ from the Cross. It's amazing as I have been a believer in the Gospel of Christ for most of my life. Just like many of us, I too have simply followed tradition without real understanding of why we do what we do. I sought the Lord for what to do this year, and I heard the still small voice say, "look at the agony and suffering of my Son on that night in the Mount of Olives." The question soon came to me, "Have we really read the Word and tried to understand why and how Jesus prayed on that night? It truly was an eyeopener for me as I had never before really dwelt on that aspect of the events of that night. We have had Maundy Thursday services where we would wash the feet of the worshippers and partake of Holy Communion. I could grasp these events as they were easily understood and could be imagined without a lot of turmoil. After all, washing the disciples' feet was a way that Jesus showed himself to be a servant of the Lord and to mankind. Partaking of Holy Communion is something that we have all, as believers in Christ, been a part of as we remember the broken body and the blood that was shed for all. During Holy Week we revisit these events as they all led up to Jesus' night in the Garden and His final agony upon the cross. But never have I ever been in a service where the attention was given to all that Jesus

V

went through in the darkness of that night in the Garden of Gethsemane. The awfulness of this night that would occur before the torture of being nailed to the cross. His torment began in that Garden for though it was a dark, sullen night, it indeed was no ordinary night.

IT STARTED IN THE GARDEN

As we open our hearts and reflect upon this night, we will see the pain, suffering and agony of our Savior before He was betrayed and arrested in Gethsemane. He knew His impending arrest which would set in motion, the chain of events that would lead Him to that awful death on the cross. After reviewing these verses of scripture, the Spirit led me to look upon the happenings on this dark, yet holy night, in Jesus' life. I know we always think of Christmas and often sing the song, "O Holy Night", reminding us of Jesus' birth. But truly I could see how this night revealed itself as "Holy" as well because Jesus made the choice to be obedient to the will of our Heavenly Father, not just for the people of His day and time, but for all of mankind for eternity's sake. Jesus is now facing His death that will be the ultimate sacrifice for all. As the Spirit was leading me, I had a burning desire to do something different on Good Friday 2021. My heart melted as I read once again the story of the Garden of Gethsemane and the events that occurred. I just felt drawn to get seven people to present as I saw it, seven specific prayers that were ushered to God on that night by our Savior. Specific ways which are examples to you and me of how we can face the hardships and trials of life knowing that God in His wisdom, truly has the plans for our lives and He will never leave nor forsake us when the hard times present themselves.

I pray that as you read this book you will find something that has made it so that you, like me, will be eternally grateful for the ultimate sacrifice Jesus Christ made for all God's children all over the world. We are living at a time where so much hatred and anger are being displayed against the believers. We must remember that we are all God's children. Don't let Christ death be just a story that you celebrate at Easter with no real thought to the suffering and shame He endured to allow us access into the Kingdom. I'm so grateful to have God as my Father, Jesus as my Savior and the Holy Spirit, who rules and reigns within me as my Counselor and Guide. I like so many other believers want to say thank you as we continue to forge on looking forward to our eternal home in Heaven.

We recognize that all of the events leading up to Resurrection Sunday are certainly significant but, the Spirit moved within me to really look at this dark yet holy night our Savior spent in the Garden of Gethsemane. The story and events of Jesus' last night in the Garden appear in all four of the Gospels Matthew, Mark, Luke and John. Each gospel writer tells how Jesus immediately leaves after the Last Supper to go to His favorite garden of prayer. Just as we have different news reporters and reporting media streams, the Apostles write their stories from their own perspective but yet, it's the same story about a night that was anything but ordinary.

JESUS FACES HIS ASSIGNMENT

As I read of the events on that night from each gospel writer, I saw in the Gospel of Luke's writing seven specific ways to pray to our Father when we are faced with serious trials, tribulations and situations. These seven specific ways of coming to the Father in prayer allow us to see how God has prepared a way for us to pray and trust Him no matter what we are facing. Jesus was now facing without a doubt, the end of His time on earth. It was time to set in motion the true understanding of why He came to earth, in other words, the reason for His birth. He was, He is and He will forever be, the only acceptable sacrifice that has obtained for you and me, the right to eternal life with our Father in Heaven.

Truly, Christmas and Easter are my most favorite holidays. I so enjoy Christmas with all its' beautiful lights, the festive gatherings, the time spent sharing in love and fellowship with family and friends. But for sure, the birth of our Savior is more important than anything else we can give or receive at Christmas. We were given the best present ever and it wasn't found under a tree. I'm so glad God loves you and me enough to share His precious Son, even to the point of death for our eternal salvation. But without Jesus' death on the old rugged cross, which we celebrate as Resurrection Sunday, our lives were all doomed to eternal death in the lake of fire. Without Jesus' divine birth, there would be no celebration on Resurrection Sunday, for what appeared to be death, was just what Jesus said, "I will rise again." Oh, how grateful I am for the scared blood of Jesus. Jesus loved you and He loved me enough to say, "not my will, but thy will be done." Jesus decided to die for you and for me...if you've ever doubted that fact, read and re-read the gospel writers stories of what happened on that dark night in the Garden of Gethsemane also known as the Mount of Olives.

We will look at each writing from the books of the Apostles, but the focus for this book is going to be on the story as written by the Apostle Luke and how I was able to see how the scriptures reflected on specific and intentional prayers. Jesus was able to go through intense pain, suffering and agony emotionally, mentally and physically prior to His betrayal and arrest. But He did not go through the horrors of the night without much prayer.

It was no ordinary night and Jesus' prayers were filled with a cry to the Father to take this heavy burden from Him. But that was not how the story was to end. Jesus had to fulfill His assignment. All of mankind's sins now rested upon His shoulders. What a burden to bear, the sins of the entire world. Jesus looked over the span of life and had you and me on His mind when He took His last breath on that cross. Heavenly Father what love you have for us as You allowed Your only begotten son to give up His life for us, even though it meant intense pain and suffering and even meant Jesus' separation from You.

I want to begin by taking a look at each of the Gospels with regard to the events that they penned on that night in the Garden.

The Gospel according to Matthew 26:26-39 NLT

36 Then Jesus went with them to the olive grove called Gethsemane, and he said, "Sit here while I go over there to pray." **37** He took Peter and Zebedee's two sons, James and John, and he became anguished and distressed. **38** He told them, "My soul is crushed with grief to the point of death. Stay here and keep watch with me."

39 He went on a little farther and bowed with his face to the ground, praying, "My Father! If it is possible, let this cup of suffering be taken away from me. Yet I want your will to be done, not mine."

40 Then he returned to the disciples and found them asleep. He said to Peter, "Couldn't you watch with me even one hour? **41** Keep watch and pray, so that you will not give in to temptation. For the spirit is willing, but the body is weak!"

42 Then Jesus left them a second time and prayed, "My Father! If this cup cannot be taken away unless I drink it, your will be done." **43** When he returned to them again, he found them sleeping, for they couldn't keep their eyes open.

44 So he went to pray a third time, saying the same things again. **45** Then he came to the disciples and said, "Go ahead and sleep. Have your rest. But look—the time has come. The Son of Man is betrayed into the hands of sinners. **46** Up, let's be going. Look, my betrayer is here!"

As we look at Matthew's view of what occurred on that dark night, we see that he states Jesus' soul was crushed even to the point of death. I'm sure we cannot begin to imagine what Jesus was feeling when He stated that

His soul is crushed even to the point of death. I found comfort as I reflected upon the scripture found in Psalms 34:18, ***"The Lord is close to the brokenhearted and saves those who are crushed in spirit."*** Jesus was feeling weary and worn thinking on what was about to occur during these last days on earth. He had done no wrong, yet He is getting ready to die a harsh, cruel death. A death that for any other human would have been impossible, beyond measure of what a human could withstand or endure. Perhaps, as we say today, Jesus was in His feelings, as each time He came back, His disciples were asleep. Jesus was about to do the most extraordinary thing ever done or that can ever be done, as He was about to give up His life for all of mankind. Jesus knows what our feelings of hurt and disappointment are as we walk through this thing called "life." Indeed, this is no time to slack off at praying, no this is one of the times you can definitely say, "if I ever needed the Lord before, I sure do need Him now." Jesus was facing the worst death any human being could or would ever face. He just wanted his beloved disciples to pray with Him but each time He came back He finds them all asleep. Do you think Peter, James and John really understood His request? The Strong Tower that they had depended on was now showing signs of His humanness as He asks the disciples to pray with Him. After all, their Teacher was always in control of every situation as He spoke to the storm, walked on water, fed the multitudes, raised the dead, caused blind eyes to see, the deaf and dumb to speak and the lame to walk. Here we find Jesus showing signs of distress and anxiety, what is going on? I'm most certain the disciples were troubled too and didn't know what to say, less what to pray. This same Savior who has been their Teacher and Healer, is now asking for prayer partners, prayer warriors to join Him as says, "My soul is crushed with grief to the point of death." Perhaps, the disciples finally hear what Jesus is saying and it brings much grief and sorrow to them. As we know many times when we are overwhelmed with anxiety of impending events and occurrences, it seems so hard to find a way to have comfort and peace in these type situations. Maybe falling asleep was an escape mechanism for the disciples as they couldn't accept what was about to happen. They knew that Jesus had spoken about his going away, could this be the time, what is happening here in the Garden of peace and comfort to the Master? Being able to sleep when faced with hardships and obstacles brings about a relief as you don't have to face the reality of what is about to happen. It's evening time, perhaps close to the bedtime hour for the disciples. Jesus reminds us that the flesh is weak as it kept succumbing to sleep...not once, not twice but three times.

Interestingly on Jesus' first return to the disciples, He calls out the Apostle Peter and asks him specifically, "Couldn't you watch with me even one hour?" Peter the bold one, always being quick with his answers and responses to Jesus. Remember Peter walked on water and when asked by Jesus, "Who do you say that I am?" answered, "You are the Messiah, the Son of the living God." (NIV) Maybe that's why Jesus called his name as He wants you and I to see that even the best of family and friends can be distracted and physically tired when we need them the most. Perhaps God is making a statement that even our "ride or die" partners can disappoint us at the time when our situations are turned upside down, at the times when we don't know which way to turn. Maybe Jesus wanted us to see firsthand and to realize the frailty of being human. We can have the best of intentions, but still not meet up to the issues, demands and needs at hand. Sometimes the reality of what we are facing indeed causes even our family and friends, to sleep on us. After all, sleep is an escape mechanism for the depressed and sad at heart. Unfortunately, sleep will not take away our problems for even Jesus had to face unsurmountable circumstances in the Garden on that dark night. His response to His impending death was to pray, pray and pray some more. I know this may sound unreasonable for many, because we look for immediate results, but the outline or plan for survival in the midst of rough and tough times has been given to us when we look at how Jesus handled the fact that His accusers, being led by his Apostle Judas, were coming for Him. Jesus himself prayed to our Heavenly Father during this agony as He wrestles with His flesh to complete the will of God. The question remains, why did Jesus specifically call Peter and question him for not being able to stay awake and pray? Maybe Jesus wanted us to realize that through it all, our Heavenly Father is who we should look to first as our source of comfort, aide and assistance. For God's Word says in

Matthew 7:7 "Ask and it shall be given you, seek and ye shall find, knock and it shall be opened unto you."

Oh, what a mighty God we serve. As we read the words of this night in Gethsemane from the gospel writers Matthew, Mark, John and Luke, none of them state that Jesus showed any anger toward the sleeping disciples. Jesus showed them love even when they were not able to fulfill His request. Jesus showed compassion towards His sleeping friends where most of us would have something to say if we were expecting our closest friends to be our assistance or aid when we are facing troubles. However, this is just another example of how great the love is from our Savior. Jesus loves you and He loves me so much and He loves with an unconditional love. That's why He was able to face His death on the cross because He knew it wasn't about Him but the precious lives of God's children. Jesus became the "scapegoat" for all the believers that we might find our way home to our Heavenly Father.

The Gospel according to Mark 14:32-42 NLT

[32] They went to the olive grove called Gethsemane, and Jesus said, "Sit here while I go and pray." [33] He took Peter, James, and John with him, and he became deeply troubled and distressed. [34] He told them, "My soul is crushed with grief to the point of death. Stay here and keep watch with me."

[35] He went on a little farther and fell to the ground. He prayed that, if it were possible, he cried out, "everything is possible for you. Please take this cup of suffering away from me. Yet I want your will to be done, not mine."

[37] Then he returned and found the disciples asleep. He said to Peter, "Simon, are you asleep? Couldn't you watch with me even one hour?[38] Keep watch and pray, so that you will not give in to temptation. For the spirit is willing, but the body is weak."

³⁹ Then Jesus left them again and prayed the same prayer as before. ⁴⁰ When he returned to them again, he found them sleeping, for they couldn't keep their eyes open. And they didn't know what to say.

⁴¹ When he returned to them the third time, he said, "Go ahead and sleep. Have your rest. But no—the time has come. The Son of Man is betrayed into the hands of sinners. ⁴² Up, let's be going. Look, my betrayer is here!"

The Gospel writer Mark also notes that Jesus doesn't take all twelve of His disciples to the Garden to pray with Him. No, He only takes Peter, James and John with Him. It appears that even Jesus had an inner circle that He would allow to be with Him to witness the miraculous works that He would perform and to be His supporters. As we look in the New Testament, we find that Jesus took these same three Disciples with Him when He went to Jarius' house to heal his daughter as He **declared that his daughter was not dead, only sleeping as written in Luke 8:49-55**. The next time we see Jesus take Peter, James and John is up on the mountain with Him in **Matthew 17:1-2, as He was transfigured before them and talked with Moses and Elijah.** Jesus chose twelve disciples, but He only takes three, Peter, James and John into the Garden with Him. The Apostle John was the only one of the four gospel writers, that was literally in the Garden that night with Jesus and His account of the story is the shortest that was written. So, it seems that we can only assume that this story was told to Matthew, Mark and Luke.

We find in the Gospel of Mark verse 38, Jesus goes on to say "Keep watch and pray, so that you will not give in to temptation. For the spirit is willing, but the body is weak." Jesus knew of man's weakness when it comes to the flesh. For yes, in our spirits we may be willing, but our mortal bodies are weak. A simple request of staying awake to pray became a difficult task. Even today we struggle to remain diligent in our prayer life and our study of God's Word. Just as we find ourselves struggling when it comes to prayer, perhaps the enemy knowing the power in prayer caused the disciples to fall asleep so that they could not be on their assignment of watching and praying along with Jesus.

Death is so solemn, so cold and maybe Jesus stating that he was going away was finally sinking into the mind and thoughts of the disciples to the point that they just couldn't deal with Him departing from them. We saw how even Jesus wept when He was in the presence of Mary and Martha as the sorrow and grief they were experiencing at Lazarus' death consumed them. Even today when we lose love ones who are near and dear to us, it is not something we easily forget and get over. Grief is such a process and it has no time limit on it. For the disciples hearing Jesus say He was going away, perhaps was something they just couldn't fathom.

As Jesus keeps coming back to the disciples, they were at a loss and just didn't know what to say. We know that their love for Jesus was genuine. They were the ones chosen by Jesus to be with Him in the Garden on that sullen night. As Mark has penned in his gospel writing, Jesus calls out to Peter asking him why he couldn't stay awake and pray. We see that Jesus doesn't call him Peter which means rock, he has called him Simon, his old name. So, here we see how easily man can fall back into his old ways. Simon's name was changed by Jesus as He had shown himself to be firm as a Rock in His relationship with Jesus. He had grown to a point that Jesus knew He could call on him and look for him to be there as a support to Him. But now, as Jesus is praying to get His heart and His mind to fully accept this assignment of becoming the blood and body that would suffer for mankind for all of eternity, He finds even the Rock sleeping on the job.

Did the disciples finally understand what Jesus was saying when He told them He would be leaving? For me, this night brings so many memories of times where we have had to say farewell on this side of heaven to our loved ones and friends. It is truly hard to say goodbye to those we love and especially when they are speaking of dying and all you want is for them to keep living. Jesus is now at the point that words meet reality. No more talking about leaving, for the soldiers are now arriving along with Jesus' betrayer. The curtain call is about to begin as the journey begins from the Garden to the Cross.

The Gospel according to John 18:1-5

18 After Jesus finished this prayer; he left with his disciples and went across the Kidron Valley to a place where there was a garden. ² Judas, the traitor, knew where this place was, for Jesus had gone there often with his disciples. ³ The Pharisees and the leading priests had given Judas a large detachment of Roman soldiers and temple police to seize Jesus. Judas guided them to the garden, all of them carrying torches and lanterns and armed *with swords and spears.* ⁴ Jesus, knowing full well what was about to happen, went out to the garden entrance to meet them. Stepping forward, he asked, "Who are you looking for?" ⁵ "Jesus of Nazareth," they replied. (Now Judas, the traitor, was among them.) He replied, "I am He."

The Apostle John as previously mentioned, has the shortest writing of the events from the night in Gethsemane. John makes note that Jesus often went to the Garden with His disciples. He gets right to the point as he tells his story from Jesus arrival in the Garden to the time that the traitor Judas, arrives with the Roman soldiers and the temple police. Also, in John's writings, we are told of how Jesus goes to the entrance of the Garden and identifies himself as Jesus of Nazareth, the one they are looking for. How bold is that? You walk out to the ones who have come to arrest you and you have not committed one crime or injustice to anyone? It's more than a notion to boldly face the enemies who have come to take you before the chief priests and the rulers, to have you charged with a crime that you never committed. After the Passover meal with Jesus and the other disciples, Judas went out to fulfill his assignment of betrayal. Jesus knowing all things, told Judas in John 13:27, **"what you are about to do, do quickly"**. Jesus knew of His approaching death and from these words we can see that He was wanting to get things over with. Judas returns to the Garden, but he does not come back alone. He leads the soldiers, and the temple police to where Jesus is. The most noted act of betrayal in all of history is now taking place. They are coming for Jesus armed with swords and spears. They are coming equipped as if they are taking into custody a thief, a robber, or a criminal of some hideous act. No, they are coming for the Savior who even though these men are arresting Him, will give up His life, even for His enemies, as they did not know who He was.

In Verse 4 we read that Jesus knew full well what was about to happen. So, He comes to the entrance and asks,

"Who are you looking for?" I can only imagine that as Jesus took each step toward the entrance of the Garden, He was having a spiritual talk with God. For who could endure so much? It had to be in this time of communing with God, that Christ was strengthened in His inner man to know that no matter what, He had a divine purpose and a high call to do what no other man could or would ever be able to do. The Bible tells us that Jesus was just an ordinary man – he didn't stand out among the crowds so that people would know Him everywhere He went. His purpose and His calling in life was never about Him – first He was born in a humble manner, in humble surroundings to serve, not to be served. Here is another example of how Jesus was obedient in all of His ways.

The Apostle John goes on to tell us in Verse 5, that the soldiers state they are looking for **"Jesus of Nazareth"**. Jesus knowing of the events that are about to unfold steps forward and replies, **"I am He."** These soldiers had no idea of the magnitude of who Jesus was. He didn't run or try to get away, He didn't hide or make them chase Him. Jesus could have changed His mind, but He didn't. Jesus knew what was to come as He was the only sacrifice that could redeem mankind. Jesus stayed the course. He did not abort his assignment and because of His unselfish love for man, He endured the bitter cross to save you and to save me. After much prayer and travail in the Garden,

Jesus sets in motion the divine calling to the cross. No matter what version you read, this night was the beginning of the end for His earthly ministry and life. Jesus knew His appointed time had come.

The Gospel according to Luke 22:39-46

As I stated earlier as I re-read these verses from the Gospel of Luke, my eyes were opened to seven specific ways of praying through agony and suffering. Seven ways that our Savior approached prayer to our Father during this hard night of mental suffering and anguish. For many of us today, it is stress that weighs us down and causes many health as well as mental issues. We have so many worries for ourselves and our families, so many problems that keep coming up and cause us to lose heart in our journey called life. When we are going through, do we remember to pray, pray and pray even the more? Do we doubt God as we don't see the answer right away, or have we learned in all things to trust God? Jesus as you will see, kept the assignment of sacrifice instead of giving in to the pain and heartache He was undergoing in the Garden on this night.

As we begin to look into the verses as penned by the Apostle Luke, God opened my eyes to see a new revelation. I was able to take a deeper look into what was really going on with Jesus as He retreated to the garden to pray. What conversation He must have been having with God as He struggled to find a different way for the story to be written. Jesus prayed, I mean truly prayed as if His life depended on it because, it did! Many times, we struggle with prayers for healing, purpose, direction, breakthroughs, heartache, and depression, just to name a few. But here in this Garden called Gethsemane, we find our Savior in all His human frailties crying out to our Heavenly Father, **"not my will, but thy will be done."** In the midst of my reading and preparing for Good Friday, I couldn't get past these eight words spoken in the Garden of Gethsemane by our Lord and Savior. This beautiful olive grove that in the past had caused Jesus to find comfort and peace as He talked with our Father, is now being portrayed as a place of agony and pain. What on any other ordinary night would have been a time of prayer and of gaining strength for His journey as He communed with the Father, on this night there was nothing ordinary about it. It truly was a different feeling on this night. What a dark, eerie feeling is filling the atmosphere. Perhaps that's why the disciples kept falling asleep. That deep dark spirit was lurking around this known place of peace, of solitude, this place where Jesus found sweet communion with the Father. For our Heavenly Father cannot reside in the presence of sin and evil.

For sin and evil carry a weight that overwhelms, disappoints, and disheartens us. Jesus himself was at the place of full acceptance of what was lying ahead for Him. Can you imagine for a moment what thoughts must have been on Jesus' mind?

Scripture Reading

Luke 22:39-46 NKJV

[39] Coming out, He went to the Mount of Olives, as He was accustomed, and His disciples also followed Him. [40] When He came to the place, He said to them, "Pray that you may not enter into temptation."

[41] And He was withdrawn from them about a stone's throw, and He knelt down and prayed, [42] saying, "Father, if it is Your will, take this cup away from Me; nevertheless not My will, but Yours, be done." [43] [a]Then an angel appeared to Him from heaven, strengthening Him. [44] And being in agony, He prayed more earnestly. Then His sweat became like great drops of blood falling down to the ground.

[45] When He rose up from prayer, and had come to His disciples, He found them sleeping from sorrow. [46] Then He said to them, "Why do you sleep? Rise and pray, lest you

enter into temptation."

Point #1 Praying in the Secret Place

³⁹ Coming out, He went to the Mount of Olives, as He was accustomed, and His disciples also followed Him.

The Bible states in Matthew 6:6, "But when you pray, go away by yourself, shut the door behind you, and pray to your Father in private. Then your Father, who sees everything, will reward you."

What a meaningful purpose and example Jesus set for us as He understood the worth of prayer in the secret place. As we seek to come to God in prayer, we must free ourselves from the hustle and bustle of life. We must find our "secret place", our "quiet place" where we can retreat from the busyness of life. Jesus even understood the need to get away to have His own private time with God. Many times, throughout the Bible you will find Jesus leaving the crowds, and even leaving His disciples as He goes to pray alone. It is essential that we all find that place with God. There must be a room, a closet, an area of your home, maybe it's found by staying in your car, radio turned off, cell phone silenced as you mediate and pray in your own private space with no interruptions and interferences. Life keeps us all way too busy and finding time on a consistent basis to develop our own personal relationships with God is essential and sorely needed. We want God to hear us, to know us as we petition Him for our cares and our concerns. God is always available for us 24/7 and we need to be intentional as we come before His throne of grace making our request known unto Him. Get away from everyone and spend some Me, Myself and I time with our Heavenly Father. If you struggle in praying, it's because you are thinking about it too much. Use the model prayer, The Lord's Prayer, to get you started but release your thoughts, your fears, your uncertainties to God. As you continue you will build up your confidence and find yourself praying as you seek to "have a little talk with Jesus", because He is the only one that can help us in our most dire of situations.

AGONY IN THE GARDEN

We must seek God by drawing near to Him and being in conversation with Him. He desires to hear how much we love Him as He inhabits the praises of His people. As Jesus was about to face all that He would endure to save mankind, He retreated to His secret place, the garden to pray to our Father. There is a hymn written by Charles Austin Miles entitled "I Come to the Garden Alone." This hymn definitely fits with the Saviors plight on that dark night in Gethsemane. For the lyrics tell us that as we come alone into the garden or our own secret place, we know we are heard because our Father walks and talks with us as He tells us that we are His own. Jesus was in a dire situation and knew that He needed His Father to be with Him, now more than ever before. As we find our secret place lets abide in it with our focus stayed on being in His presence. There is fullness of joy in the presence of God. No matter what you are facing just know that God's presence is found in the "secret place." Jesus knew to abide in God in a secret place. Where is it that you find that perfect place, area, spot to go before the Father? A lot of the time we if you are like me, I like to sit by the ocean and mediate on the splendor and beauty of our God. I also find peace and solace in the quiet of my home, especially in my office where I spend a lot of my time. It's there that I can fill the atmosphere with my essential oils and my gospel music of praise. Sometimes I just let the classical music as well as the gospel jazz and instrumental music play. But for sure, I understand getting to the place where you feel His presence with you as you pray. Jesus knew where to find peace in the presence of our Father. So, where is your secret place of prayer? Think about this and know that there is no right or wrong place as we go before our Father. It's all about finding that sweet communion with Him that matters the most. That feeling of knowing you have been in His presence is so fulfilling and its moments like this that are priceless. The Word of God tells us to abide in Him and He will abide in us. We have to make every effort to be in His presence for that's where we will find the peace and happiness that we need to face our adversities. There is nothing like getting into that secret place with God so that you can feel the anointing that will take over your mind, your heart and your total being. It's in the moments like this that all your cares of this world are released as you enter into the Holy place of His presence. **Psalm 100:4 reminds us to "Enter into His gates with thanksgiving and into His courts with praise; be thankful unto Him and bless His name."** When we come before the Father in our "secret place", that is indeed where we will rest in the peace and power of His presence.

Point #2 Prayer of Temptation

⁴⁰There he told them, "Pray that you will not give into temptation."

Oh my, this is a big one, "that you will not give into temptation." Wow, the very thing that got us in trouble from the beginning of time. The very thing that caused Eve to eat of the forbidden fruit is now being asked of the disciples as they are set aside and asked to pray for and with our Messiah. Temptation deals with the weakness of man's flesh. Even today, we find ourselves tempted on every hand by all sorts of evil desires of the flesh as well as the worldly desires of wealth and notoriety that are continuing to lead us into sin and damnation. We are often reminded of the fact that sin looks good, tastes good and feels good but it is not good for you. We have to know the Word which tells us that in **Romans 7:18 "I know that nothing good lives in me, that is in my flesh (my sinful nature). For I have the desire to do what is good, but I cannot carry it out."** In other words, in our flesh dwells no good thing. In our flesh is the old man, the old nature with its' passions and desires. So, we are the only ones who can take control of our sinful nature and nobody said it would be easy, but it is doable. Unfortunately for some, it has even led to premature death. We have gotten to a place where we are more concerned with what our desires are for ourselves than in remembering the ultimate cost that was paid on the cross for all mankind. We have become proud, arrogant, selfish and all about me, myself and what I want. We have forgotten to be grateful and thankful to our Heavenly Father for all that Jesus did to allow us eternal life. We seem to have forgotten the sacrifice made for us that we might live a life of righteousness and holiness unto God. We have been given His word which even lets us know in **1 Corinthians 10:13b "But when you are tempted, He will also provide a way out so that you can endure it."(NIV)** this is just another example of how much we are loved by our Savior. A way of escape, a way out will be provided, but will we be spiritual enough to take it or will be succumb to the pleasures of flesh which so easily get us tangled up in places, people and things that we need not get involved with. So because we are heirs to the throne as God's children, we need not ever forget we are saved by the redeeming blood of Jesus Christ. It is by God's grace and mercy that we have been afforded the opportunity to accept Jesus as the Lord of our lives.

We must remember to keep our flesh under control at all times reminding ourselves of who we are and whose we are. We must be the salt of the earth, the light in darkness, the hands that help, the hearts that love, the feet that bring peace wherever we go. By faith, we have authority over our flesh and have the ability to walk in victory as sons and daughters of our Most High God. Let your flesh know who is in control as you walk in faith seeking deliverance from the sin issues that plaque your life.

Point #3 Praying with Power

^{41} He walked away, about a stone's throw, and knelt down and prayed

Here we see that Jesus didn't go far away from where the disciples were. It simply says He went a stone's throw away. That's doesn't sound like it's very far at all. I'm a person who loves to praise God and as such, when I am in those places where I have heavy issues that I need to pray about, I will sometimes sing songs of praise as I invoke God's presence. Nowhere in the Bible does it state that Jesus sang hymns of praise unto God. As I pondered on that thought, I thought the reason would be that He is the song of praise wrapped in humanity. Maybe Jesus was able to hear the angels singing, Jesus had such a high spiritual calling that He indeed could think a thought and the angels would minister to Him. Having said that, Jesus knew what praying with power meant. Jesus was part of the Trinity and was in the beginning and will be with us in the end. He understood the Power that was able to be released through the Holy Ghost. He knew who to call on as His time was drawing nigh. He was able to be comforted by angels as I can only imagine the impending thoughts of the upcoming events were playing over and again in His mind. It's hard enough to know that you are facing death but to have to be tormented, bruised, abused, spat on, ridiculed in the process, I am sure was overwhelming to our Savior. But Jesus knew where to draw the strength that was needed to overcome this agony. When we look at **Psalm 107:28, "Then they cried to the LORD in their trouble, and he delivered them from their distress.",** we know that Jesus knew that God would deliver Him from the distress that He was experiencing. God is our loving Father and even though Jesus was given this horrific assignment, it was for the purpose of saving mankind until eternity. He stayed on His assignment in spite of the impending pain and suffering. What indescribable love was given for you and me as we now can truly understand the cost of the cross. Prayer is a powerful weapon as God gives us strength to endure what seems impossible in and of ourselves. We must realize that the power of prayer resides in the God who is being prayed to. **1 John 5:14-15 tells us, "This is the confidence we have in approaching God: that if we ask anything according to his will, he hears us. And if we know**

**that he hears us - whatever we ask - we know that
we have what we asked of him."**

Praying with power takes us to higher heights in our
devotion and love of God. We must no longer be like the
babes still sucking milk. No, we have matured to the point
that we are now at the table eating the meat. In other
words, our spiritual walk has us knowing how to go to
God in fervent, effectual prayer. We know how to pray in
our "heavenly language" with no shame. We understand
how to pray in the spirit and sometimes to just get in His
presence through song and praise. Praying with power
means we understand "by any means necessary" we will
seek the Lord's presence. We are going to pray until His
presence saturates our hearts and our minds. We are
going to pray until we go from sitting to kneeling to falling
prostrate before our Father. Praying with power means we
give God 100%. There is an acronym that is so inspiring
for praying with power. It is from the word PUSH. **P**ray
Until **S**omething **H**appens. When our prayers align with
God's will for our lives, nothing can stop us from receiving
answered prayers of what God has for us. Power is what
rose Jesus up out of that grave and that same power is
available for the believers, if we have relationship with our
Father. He wants us to be obedient and to live a holy and
righteous life before Him. All we need is the Holy Ghost
power that lies within us to be alive and working. You want

power, you need to pray and ask God for it. We pray for our family problems, for our health, for wealth, for jobs, cars, homes, etc., but how many of us pray to God for an increased spiritual life? For the power to be used by God as change agents for such a time as this? Do we think of ways that we can use even our meager resources to be a blessing to others? Being used by God in effective prayer, in ways such as an intercessory prayer leader or a prayer partner, as a watchman on the wall, is so needed in today's time. Are you willing to make the sacrifice to give God your all for whatever you put your hands to for the Kingdom? It all begins with effectual prayer as God will hear our request. Our hearts desire should always be, Father I want to do more for You. We need to pray and ask God for more of His wisdom, knowledge and understanding so that as we come to Him in prayer, our prayers will become that sweet smelling savor that is pleasing to His nostrils. As we spend more time with God praying effective and fervent prayers, we will then know more of how to speak with authority declaring those things that are not as if they are. How many of us, are truly seeking and asking God for the ability to dwell more in the spiritual realm than in the worldly things we see around us? For in the natural we see all kinds of things that are good and desirable but if we would take a moment and pause and reset, asking God what His plan is for us, we would see in the Spirit realm that what we want, is not always within the will of

God. Every denial is not always a final "NO". Sometimes it's just a delay until God finishes a work within us or has a better plan than ours. Being consistent in prayer like Jesus was, helps us to get in His presence and pray with power knowing that God only wants what's best for you and for me. We must be able to look past our current situation to the ability that we have through God to rise above what we see as we draw strength from the spirit realm knowing that God is our Helper, our Deliverer, our Sustainer and our Restorer. Pray with power to believe that all things are possible with God, because guess what, it is.

Point #4 Prayer of Submission

[42] "Father, if you are willing, please take this cup of suffering away from me. Yet I want your will to be done, not mine."

Here we find Jesus making the ultimate sacrifice to give up His will so that our Heavenly Father's will can be done. Why do I say sacrifice? Because just like you and me, Jesus had a choice to obey or disobey. Jesus is showing us how we must be obedient to the Father out of our love for Him. We must want to serve Him and understand that God wants us to submit to His will just like Jesus did on this dark night. His love for our Father is shown over and again in Jesus' life as He always gives glory to God. This cup Jesus was about to endure was a heavy one as He would take on himself the very wrath from God that we deserve for our sins. This makes it very clear why we see Jesus praying, "take this cup from me?" Jesus makes His appeal to God, but He understands that God's will is first and His is secondary. Jesus shows us an example of true submission as He submits, yields to and surrenders His will to the Father's decision.

Too many times we find ourselves struggling with the will of God. We want things the way we think it should be and fail a lot of the time, to seek our Father for His will for whatever we are facing. Here we see by example that even the Son of God, asked God for advice while facing a difficult situation. This was a pinnacle point in Jesus' life as He had always been in total fellowship with God, the Holy Spirit and was able to call on a myriad of angels anytime He wanted. But now, time has met with the calling on Jesus' life. His life is now to be given up as the only perfect sacrifice to save mankind. Submission gets a lot of us in trouble as we feel it is a negative thought. But in all honesty, if we are not willing to submit, how can we be obedient to what the will of our God is for us? Too often, we look at submission as something that is wrong as we feel someone wants to make us a slave to them and have us agree with them on everything. Submitting in the right way, brings peace in the midst of chaos and joy to those affected by it. As Jesus was able to submit to God, He has afforded us a life far beyond measure as His willingness to die for you and me, has gained us life eternal with our Heavenly Father instead of life eternal in that fiery pit known as Hell. I thank Jesus for submitting His will to the Father's on our behalf. We should always remember how the joy that Jesus affords us is way beyond what we see as joy in the natural. The joy that is afforded you and me, is unspeakable as it is something that this world knows nothing about and can't take away from us.

Jesus, because of His divine nature, was able to see what was going to happen to Him. We have the benefit of honoring Jesus as He cared enough for you and me to take this bitter cup and die for all of mankind, for we may not have seen Jesus in our lives but we believe this Word called the Bible which tells us of the Way, the Truth and the Life. He didn't have to do it, but He did. His love of the Father was so great that in spite of all the pain and torture He would endure, He was obedient unto death. Jesus had to finally accept that which He knew and understood was going to be a vile and horrific death. He yielded himself to the will of the highest in authority, God. He could have discussed with God another way to save mankind, but instead He submitted His will to the Fathers. He submitted himself wholly to God's ultimate plan for mankind. Too many times today, submission is misused and abused. No, submission is not wrong for submitting as we Jesus' example here, means coming in agreement to make things work for the best for others and allowing our wills to be forfeited as we see the larger plan that God has. We should treat each other with mutual respect, love, decency and honor. Jesus gave God his total submission, "not my will, but your will be done." Let our love for one another cause us to be totally committed to each other in accepting that having things always operate in our will of what we want, is not always the way things will work out. No one can compare to the great love that Jesus has for us as He lived in perfect submission to God. He chose to enter this sinful world, give up His life on the cross so that He could become the ultimate sacrifice for sin, once and for all. No more blood offerings, nothing else would be needed as the atonement for sin. **Philippians 2:6-7 reminds us that (Jesus Christ) [6] who, being in the form of God, did not consider it robbery to be equal with God, [7] but made Himself of no reputation, taking the form of a bondservant, *and* coming in the likeness of men.** Being able to submit shows a sign of obedience as submission keeps you humble. There is nothing any worse than persons who are always right, have to have their way about everything, are not a team player but yet want to boss everyone around and the persons who are quick to argue their point whether right or wrong. Yes, it takes great humility to not have your say all the time, nor your way all the time. Submission means you are more interested in making things work for the common good of everyone instead of making sure you get noticed or called out with praise for what you have done. Only God can really transform people from disobedience to obedience as people have to submit their selfish ways to ways that will bring peace and harmony for the common good.

Point #5 Prayer for Strength

⁴³ Then an angel from heaven appeared and strengthened him. ⁴⁴ He prayed more fervently.

Here in this verse we see that as soon as Jesus prays "yet not my will but yours be done," an angel appeared and strengthened Him. Even Jesus being human and Divine was able to be ministered to by an angel. This gives us an example of how when God has a plan for you and me, He will give you the strength to do what you never thought you could or would do. The angel appeared from heaven and provided strength for Jesus. After having finally submitted His will, His acceptance of being obedient even unto death, was realized. This is a hard thing to accept even today as we face severe illness, the spiraling effects of alcohol and drug abuse and even death. It takes supernatural strength to be able to face these obstacles and to believe by faith that God will deliver what it is we are praying for. How many times have we stood by the beside of someone who is transitioning from this side of heaven? How many times have you had family or friends have to deal with cancer, kidney failure, diabetes and the list goes on? Jesus in His humanness knows what it is to face death even though you are not really prepared mentally. Can you imagine what He must have felt as He played over and again in His mind the impending suffering, shame and ultimate pain He would experience? Praying for strength requires the ability to withstand great pressure, it draws on our ability to be tough and firm while going through much pain and suffering, emotionally, mentally and physically.

The angel came to strengthen Jesus but look at what the next line of scripture states, "He prayed more fervently." The definition of fervent means to exhibit particular enthusiasm, zeal, conviction, persistence, or belief; and to have or show emotional passion. Jesus had to trust our Father even more as He had to endure so much before He would rejoin Him in eternity. The angel I'm sure brought a sense of peace, love and comfort to Jesus that was beyond man's ability. Jesus was convicted to complete His assignment even though it was a hard and painful one. He did this for you and for me...truly what love.

When I think of strength, I think of the ability to get the energy and the willpower to do what I may not want to do. When I am faced with something that I do not have the ability to do in my own strength, that's when I have learned to pray even more. This is where Jesus was on that night. He for a moment, was contemplating whether or not there could be a better way to save mankind. Jesus was seeking for a moment to see if there was anything else that could occur to fulfill His assignment without so much pain and suffering. In my own lifetime I have had to endure some hardships that bought me to my knees in prayer. I've had to face the death of not one, but both my sons through the issues that drug use and abuse caused them physically and mentally. I can understand why the text tells us that Jesus prayed even more fervently as He had to deal with unbearable pain thinking of what was ahead. Too many times, during the lives of my sons, I prayed over and again for total deliverance so that I would not have to face their deaths before mine. But God, knowing all things did not write the script another way for me. Just like Jesus faced terrible agony on this night, our Father knows our beginning and our end and definitely knows the plans for each of our lives, so much better than we ever could.

In this frail moment in time the angel had to remind Jesus of what this sacrifice of His life was going to mean for all of mankind. In His humanness, Jesus was at a point where He needed to be strengthened. We can only imagine how Jesus must have felt as the pain that awaited Him was going to be so great. I'm sure He must have felt that all He wanted was to end this impending suffering that was ahead of Him. This is a hard moment for any believer as moments like this can bring you to your lowest point as you question, God is there another way? Jesus kept it real and He is letting you and me know, that it's ok to let God know how you really feel. Tell Him all about your feelings in the good and especially in the rough and tough times. For He understands and is so loving that His grace and mercy will cover you as He holds you and me in His loving arms, providing hope, faith and belief that He is working everything out for our good. That's what Jesus understood as He gathered the strength needed to face His death. He was about to die the type of death that was afforded for robbers and murderers yet, He had never sinned. Surely, Jesus didn't deserve to die in this horrific manner. However, we all must remain grateful that Jesus was willing to live in obedience to the will of our Father as He took the sins of the whole world upon His shoulders. He strengthened Himself to do what was impossible for any other human to do.

Point #6 Praying through Suffering

And he was in such agony of spirit that his sweat fell to the ground like great drops of blood.

Unfortunately, suffering, painful events, distress and death of our loved ones and friends is something that we all will go through in life. In our humanness we have seen suffering with illness, physically and mentally and we suffer when relationships end with someone that we thought we would build our future with or maybe we are suffering because of abuse, physical and mentally, lack of employment, decent housing, or not having been raised by both parents. Indeed, the list could go on and on of the many ills that beset the believer today. It seems that when we suffer, we try to numb our feelings instead of dealing with them. I have found that when you get to the place that yes, it hurts, yes I'm upset that I have to go through this, yes, I am angry about the death of my loved one, when you can face

Apostle Dr. Barbara Maybin Wise, Th.D

up to your feelings, that's when the healing can begin. In other words, we have to learn to "own our feelings" so that we can be healed. Jesus cried out to the Father and came to Him in humbleness as He bowed down and prayed that this cup of sorrow might pass Him by. When we look at this example of suffering, we find the Son, asking if at all possible, can this cup of suffering be taken away? Jesus knew what was facing him. He realizes that He cannot escape the pain and death that awaited Him. Jesus being divine and human knew He was getting ready to embark on the human frailties that would cause Him much suffering and pain. Jesus knew He could not escape this journey, so He went into prayer. Prayer to help him in His weakness to be able to endure the cross, its shame and its suffering. What a loving Savior we serve for He went past the pain and suffering to see the hearts of His children and the need for a Redeemer to open the gates of heaven for all. Truly no one else could have taken on this assignment. Jesus in His love for you and me, gave up His life to save many. Even those who were not His friends, those who made fun of Him, spit on Him, struck Him with a spear in His side, He died for His enemies as well as those who loved Him and cared about Him. God cares that all of His children would be saved and His son, Jesus carried this same sentiment when He walked that path to

44

the cross with all its shame and degradation. There is no measure to the suffering that Jesus endured. His suffering and the agony of knowing what was to happen I'm sure was hard to bear. But He was able to strengthen Himself in the power and might of the God-man that would truly become the ultimate sacrifice forever of mans' sins. As we look at **Isaiah 53:4-5 "Surely He took up our infirmities and carried our sorrows. He was pierced for our transgressions, He was crushed for our iniquities; the punishment that brought us peace was upon Him, and by His wounds we are healed."** Jesus Christ indeed was the Suffering Servant, sent on His mission by God to redeem mankind according to the will of our Father. Now we can see that God sent His Son into the world to suffer and die so that we can know how deep God's love is towards us. Let us not forget, **John 3:16 "For God so loved the world that He gave His only Son, so that everyone who believes in Him shall not perish but have eternal life."** Jesus' suffering was for the greater gain as He opened the portals to allow you and me to have life everlasting as we can now go to God on our own. No more burnt offerings of sacrifice, Jesus was and will forever be the Suffering Servant who gave His life for all of mankind for evermore.

Point #7 Prayer of Forgiveness

⁴⁵ At last he stood up again and returned to the disciples, only to find them asleep, exhausted from grief. ⁴⁶ "Why are you sleeping?" he asked them. "Get up and pray, so that you will not give in to temptation."

As we read this story from the Gospel of Luke, we see he only mentions Jesus returning to His disciples once to ask, why are they sleeping. However, Mark and Matthew both say that Jesus returned three times and found them asleep each time. Jesus was facing an undeserved death and He was simply asking His beloved disciples to pray so that they would not give in to temptation. Jesus was advising them of the events that would soon be unfolding. He wanted them to understand how they were going to be tempted in the flesh as He moves forward with the plans of giving up His life on the cross. Jesus knew that Peter would deny him, He knew that the disciples would run and here we find him letting the disciples know how weak the flesh is as we have a difficult time not allowing temptations to cause us to slip and fall. Jesus had told them earlier that same night as written in Matthew 26:31, "This very night you will all fall away on account of me, for it is written: 'I will strike the shepherd, and the sheep of the flock will be scattered.' In this same chapter Verse 33 we find Peter boldly replied, "Even if all fall away on account of you, I never will." Jesus knew the truth that they all would deny him as they were frightened and didn't know what to do to help the Master. Now we can perhaps understand why Jesus called Peter out as being asleep as well. He had just told the Master at the Last Supper prior to their going into the Garden, how he would never fall away from Him, how he would never deny Him even if others did. Jesus had the three go further into the Garden with Him so that they might pray and not give into temptation. Jesus was speaking of their weakness of the flesh as each time He returns they are asleep. The disciples were not ready to accept what was about to occur. After all Jesus always had the answers, He was always solving the issues at hand whether it be healing, casting out demons, feeding the hungry or teaching by parables. Why are you sleeping, Jesus asks the disciples? Jesus had simply asked them to watch and pray which seems like a simple assignment. Jesus is concerned as they will deny Him and He knows that they could possibly be led into other sins once He gets arrested. Sin so easily besets mankind and our Savior shows his love as He is not scolding the disciples because they are sleeping, He is simply trying to warn them of what is going to occur and how our flesh will respond. None of the readings from the Gospels of this night in Gethsemane tell us that Jesus became angry with the disciples for falling asleep. Jesus is gentle and kind in His approach. He is a forgiving God who looks beyond our faults to see our needs. What love Jesus shows for His disciples. Many times, when we put our trust in family and friends to be with us through thick and thin, we look around and they are not there. We get upset, some people will cut you off their list and have nothing to do with you. There may be others who will share a few choice words with you for not being there, but not Jesus. He loves us in spite of our shortcomings, in spite of our feeble attempts. Jesus loves you and He loves me and that's why even though the cross was a bitter cup to swallow, Jesus did it because of His love and desire to save us.

Jesus knew everything so why now would He be saying that His disciples would fall away? He was speaking of the fear that would grip them as they saw the fierce attack upon him. Fear of the unknown has caused the failure of so many believers as just when the breakthrough or the change is about to happen, our minds take us back to the unknown with its' many uncertainties. I'm sure it was not easy and that the disciples were fearful of their lives and the association that they had with Jesus. Denying Jesus was the easy way out. The way that they could escape death as they didn't know if they would be beaten or possibly killed because of Jesus. Fear takes a hold of our emotions and will cause us to easily move into staying with what we know, taking care of ourselves and never taking that step by faith as we, launch forward to see what God has in store for us. It will take us away from concerns for others as we fear our own existence and meaning. We all need to ask forgiveness as we have fallen short of truly moving by faith, not by sight. We must believe the Word that says God is with us, desires the best for us and will never see us forsaken nor begging for bread.

Jesus' struggle in the Garden of Gethsemane was over. Again, we can say, "It is finished." Jesus was finally accepting the fate that was ahead of him knowing that He had completed the works that God had for Him in His natural life. We are told in Matthew and in the Gospel of Mark that Jesus says, **"Let's be going, look my betrayer is here"**. Judas is on his way with the temple police and soldiers to betray Jesus. You would think that Judas would have ran away after pointing Jesus out to the police and soldiers. But oh no, our Savior was betrayed with a kiss, a sign of affection and love for one another was now being seen as a sign of death. Judas had fulfilled his assignment and had received his money for the betrayal. As sad as this scenario is, it was all within the plan that God had from the beginning of time. A Savior would come into the world to save mankind from eternal death in hell. Jesus had prayed and prayed until He was without a doubt sure of what it was that He would have to do. He had lived a sinless, holy and righteous life and was able to accept the fact that His birth and His death was a divine assignment from our Heavenly Father. It's because of Jesus' unselfish life and His ultimate sacrifice, that we are saved and able to spend eternity in Heaven with our Father.

Finally, as we look at **Hebrews 9:26-28** we read: **"But now He has appeared once for all at the end of the ages to do away with sin by the sacrifice of himself. Just as man is destined to die once, and after that to face judgment, so Christ was sacrificed once to take away the sins of many people; and he will appear a second time, not to bear sin, but to bring salvation to those who are waiting for him."** For that we give God a praise as Jesus death was unmerited. Isn't it good to know that we are genuinely loved by our Heavenly Father?

We cannot thank our God enough for loving us so much. The Word tells us in **1 John 4:9-10 "This is how God showed his love among us: He sent his only begotten**

Son into the world that we might live through him. This is love: not that we loved God, but that He loved us and sent his Son as an atoning sacrifice for our sins." What a Holy and sacred night we see in the Garden as this indeed was no ordinary night. It was a night full of agony, suffering and pain. Just as Jesus was born in Bethlehem, we can see from this erie night, that his birth had to occur in order for His death to bring eternal life. For this we are eternally grateful forevermore.

CONCLUSION

What a story has been told in that Garden of Gethsemane. One of unbelievable pain and suffering that was physically and mentally expressed by Jesus. As I read and re-read these verses, I truly understand why He also has the title of the Suffering Servant. I only thought of this title as He suffered so much on the cross, but His suffering started on this night of agony in Jesus' favorite place to pray. Doesn't that seem odd, that the very place you go to find solace and rest, now has become the place that the beginning of the end, unfolds for our Savior. But His suffering was for your benefit and for mine. This is true love, undeniable love, undeserving love, but yet a completed love that now finds Jesus seated at the right hand of our Father in Heaven, interceding on our behalf. I pray this book will remind you that Christ death should not be a story to just celebrate at Easter with no thought to the suffering and shame He endured to allow us access into the Kingdom. I truly want to like so many other believers, say "Thank you Jesus" for giving up your life for me and all of mankind. Jesus has paved the way for eternal life, and we need not fear or worry about the coldness, or the pain that comes with death, for because of His death, we can live forever. Hallelujah, to the Lamb of God!

About the Author

Apostle Dr. Barbara Maybin-Wise, holds a Doctorate degree in Theology from the Christian Education Theological Institute & Seminary of Charleston, SC and a Masters' Degree in Christian Counseling from Family Bible Seminary of Baltimore Maryland. She has spent over 48 years in service and ministry to others and officially accepted her call to ministry on November 13, 2005. She was the Founder and Senior Pastor of Always Abiding in God Ministry for 16 years.

She has been involved with and supported many outreach projects including feeding of the homeless and shelters for abused and displaced women as well as support of prison ministries throughout the Baltimore/DC region. She has worked along with, The Helping Up Mission in Baltimore City; Grassroots, Sara's House, Hope Works and The Gospel Rescue Mission of DC.

www.ingramcontent.com/pod-product-compliance
Lightning Source LLC
Chambersburg PA
CBHW070942120626
46546CB00004B/1530